I am not Writing a Book of Poems in Hawaii

Rick Lupert

Oahu, Hawaii

I am not Writing a Book of Poems in Hawaii

Ain't Got No Press

Design, Layout, Photography ~ Rick Lupert
Author Photo ~ Addie Lupert

First Edition ~ August, 2022

ISBN-13: 978-1-7330278-2-3

Visit the author online at
www.PoetrySuperHighway.com

No one has family in Hawaii. Everyone is family in Hawaii.

- Richie Norton

I thought my book was done, then we went to Hawaii and the whole last chapter happened.

- Mariel Hemingway

Hawaii is the only place I know where they lay flowers on you while you are alive.

- Will Rogers

Thank you Addie, Jude, Brendan, Elizabeth, The Thread, Jack, the singing fish, and everyone in Hawaii who uses the word *family* like they mean it.

The poem "Factual Facts" (page 11) first appeared in Oddball Magazine, May 31, 2022

The poems "Land" (page 36) and "At the Nutridge Luau" (page 111) first appeared in *Dashboard Horus,* February 21, 2022

*For Addie who embarassed the Hawaiian flowers because,
I mean, come on man, look at her...*

Before Fly

Expectations

I
We're heading to Hawaii tomorrow.
It's a shorter trip and I don't think I'll
get a whole book of poems out if it,
so I'm not really sure where
I'm going with this.

II
We're heading to Hawaii tomorrow.
I assume the airplane will be
made out of pineapple.

We're In This Together

We picked up our son from camp yesterday.
So those of you used to these books beginning
with us dropping our son off at camp
I assure you, I'm just as confused
as you are.

Factual Facts

We're heading to Hawaii tomorrow.
Hawaii is an island, or more factually,
Hawaii is a collection of islands.
That is most of the factual information
I can provide at this time.

I will tell you that when I think of
being on an island, I think of the
television show *Lost* which was
set on an island on which a lot of
crazy things happened.

As another piece of factual information
the island we are going to happens
to be where *Lost* was filmed, so
we expect a lot of crazy things
will happen.

Parenting Lessons from the Holy One

Do not say to yourself... "Because of my righteousness,
God has brought me to possess this land...
    Deuteronomy 9:4

We brought our kid to Jewish camp two weeks ago.
We armed him with all the socks he could need, face masks
in his preferred color, and every essential one could
need in the wilderness.

All we asked was that he write us postcards
even just one, so we had a sense that he was alive.
We wrote him by the system provided every single day,
but our trips to the mailbox proved fruitless.

We made it so easy...the postcards already stamped
and with our address on them. They were tiny too,
barely space to write three words
He could have written *I am alive.*

Even sent back a blank postcard and he could
tell us later he thought we were psychic.
I would have found that hilarious! But now,
less than a week before we pick him up

and we don't even know if he'll still be there,
we'll dutifully show up. We'll pile his dirt
into our trunk. We'll take him to brunch.
We'll take him to goddammed Hawaii.

We won't do these things to reward righteous behavior
but because this is what he has been promised.
This is our obligation as parents. We would bring him
to the wilderness, and then carry him

back across the river to his promised land.
This is how the Israelites got across their river
despite decades of complaining and a golden calf,
despite rebellions and broken tablets.

The Parent of all parents would not leave
His children in the desert.
and neither will we.

Expectation

There is a lot of expectation being
communicated to me on social media

where I have now revealed I'm going
to Hawaii, to write a book on this trip.

As I mentioned (though you may have missed it
if you skipped right to this page) this is a shorter trip

so I'm trying to write most of it the night before we leave.
I still don't have great confidence that

I'm going to be able to pull this off.
In fact, the next poem I write will be called

*Sorry, Folks, I'm not Writing a Book of Poems
in Hawaii.*

Sorry, Folks, I'm Not Writing a Book of Poems in Hawaii.

So if this
appears
on a page
in a book
that you
are reading,
I insist you
question
everything.

That Last Poem

with a maximum of three words
on each line, is for Ross Wolman
who now appears in two of my books
and who is forever wondering why
I break my lines
when I do.

Hawaiiku

There should be a poetry form
called the *Hawaiiku* developed
for occasions like this.
It's three lines written
on a pineapple.

This poem is clearly not
a Hawaiiku.

Hawaiiku Too

That's right, spellcheck
Hawaiiku...
I am in control here.

There Are Pineapples in Hawaii

A man on the internet almost ruined everything
by telling me there were no more pineapples in Hawaii
but then I went to the other part of the internet
and found out there were, but they're not
originally from there. I don't know what to
think anymore.

Impossibly Cute

Addie spent the better part of the day deciding which bags to bring with us. Perhaps you're a bag person too and you understand what this is all about. Towards the end of the day I asked her if we needed a special bag just for our vaccination cards, which may have been too far and led to her storming into the room where I was with an angry-ish, but impossibly cute *what did you just ask me?!*

I'm tired.

Tired like this trip has already happened.
Tired with the weight of a five thirty a.m.
      ride-on-demand.
I'm tired of masks and all the hours
      I'm about to wear them.
I should sleep, but we all know
      that's not going to happen.

I'm the first guy to say

is that the one with the round ball
whenever someone brings up sports
I tell Jay in Chicago who may wonder
why I'm messaging him at too early in the morning.
I'm heading to Hawaii, Jay.
We've gone over this.
But, like I'm telling everybody,
don't expect a book of poems
out of this. Now turn the page everybody.
Nothing to see here.

Uber (Or Lyft...I Don't Remember)

I
The fog in the Sepulveda Pass –
It's almost as if Los Angeles
doesn't want us to leave.

II
Who's ready for
a lot of commentary
about how I'm going to
lose my phone
in a volcano?

III
Our driver used to be our mailman.
He still uses that pronoun.

Or at least he was the mail *person.*
I'm making adjustments

for our new house.
which he may know better than we do.

He likes our hill.
He only drives on Tuesdays

and sorts mail in Burbank
the rest of the week.

The way his Prius bobs up and down
in the carpool lane

makes it almost impossible
to document this.

IV
Everyone's got the same story
I only do this part time
as we leave the freeway
at Howard Hughes Parkway –
Or is it an *avenue*?
I need to do my research.
Driving people from here to there
is just a cultural experiment I do
to pass the time between
sorting the mail
and living my best life.

LAX

I
I've never heard of some of these airlines.
So much has happened since the
plague descended.

II
There are plenty of donuts at Dunkin'
unlike that debacle in Syracuse
five books ago which got a whole
book named after it despite the fact
that it was a book of poems
about New Orleans.

Plane-pool

The plane next to us is going to Maui.
We're Honolulu bound.

There's something to be said
about plane-pooling.

We have wrist bands which
will tell them on the ground over the ocean

we have filled out all the paperwork
and had all the shots.

This will expedite our transition
into the *ho-lei* land.

There is vegan sushi in our future
and maybe a volcano.

Hawaiiku

Hawaiian Airlines
planes are more beautiful than
American ones

American

I
They're not using the right words
Telling us that there is no WiFi on the flight.
There is WiFi, just no internet.
This will be noted in the final report.

II
No internet on the flight
which, I imagine, is how
cavemen used to fly.

III
Can you still say *cavemen*
or is it *cave people* now?

Take Off

I
This new phone case has a texture which
makes it difficult to pull out of my pocket.
I'm pretty sure the friction is going to rip off
my pants the next time I have to answer a text.
Aloha!

II
A toddler does a countdown to takeoff
but this airline is not on her schedule
and when she reaches zero nothing happens.
This is her first lesson.

III
This airplane is equipped with
larger overhead bins. I may take a nap
in one of them. Use caution though.
I may shift positions during flight.

IV
Welcome to the sky, Addie says.
Welcome to this book, Addie.

Hawaiiku

The pilot says we
can take naps, watch movies and
do the things you do.

The Donut King

I watch *The Donut King* on the plane –
The story of the Cambodian refugee who

came to America penniless and started a
donut empire which fueled the success

of many of his country-people who still own
most of the donut shops in California.

He lost most of his money gambling and the
last bit was stolen by the CHP.

He moved back to Cambodia and
wants to live a simple life now.

Seventy seven years old, his American dream
lost in the desert.

In Flight

Gone are the
pre-pandemic
inflight magazines
of our youth.

The high pitched shrieks
of the inflight toddler
from tarmac to tarmac
help me remember just
how alive I am.

Yes, lady behind me,
with your constant
adjustments and jiggling
in the seat back in front of you
which is, coincidentally,
the one behind me,
you are alive too!
Mazal tov!

Land

We are leaving 32,000 feet behind
for space below these clouds.

All I see is ocean but the pilot
is confident we are a half hour away

from Daniel K. Inouye International Airport
where our luggage and a *SpeediShuttle* await.

I didn't pay extra for the lei greeting
as it seemed gratuitous and there

are numerous luaus in our future.
Finally one of the islands appears

to the left of the plane. *Molokai* –
evidence this whole thing isn't a dream.

If we time it right we could be
eaten by a volcano.

This One Gets Its Own Page

I
Addie's most significant contribution
to any book so far is suggesting the first chapter
of this book should be called *Waikiku*.

II
The plane touches the ground.
Aloha Addie says. She knows
Just what to say.

III
I would like to report we have
landed in Hawaii so we don't have
a *Lost* situation on our hands.

The Bathrooms at the Daniel K. Inouye International Airport

The *men* and *women* symbols
are dressed in Hawaiian outfits.
Our aloha journey begins right here
in the airport.

Hawaiiku

The *SpeediShuttle*
gets it's name for reasons I
cannot comprehend.

An Afternoon in Hawaii

Question nothing

I tell Addie as she questions
her diet choices juxtaposed

against the variety of piña coladas
available at the restaurant.

She's got an Addie's eye view
of the drinks as the bar tender

leis them on the counter for
other diners. *Ooh there's a blue one*

she squeals giving in to the
desires of her heart.

A Person Must Eat

My double jointed twelve year old
holds out his oddly shaped elbow
and says *daddy look I broke my arm*
hovering over a taro-based veggie burger
and a fruit plate with mediocre fruit
but with a pineapple cream dipping sauce
that is to die for. Wait, what was I talking about?

Jude Will be Writing the Rest of This Book.

Jude discovers a pineapple shaped fan
in a store and says look it's a *fanapple*
I couldn't be more proud, as a parent, of
what he has accomplished here today.

Hawaiicalypse

The towel stands
at the Hilton Hawaiian Village
are out of towels.
End of days.
End of days.

If I'd known

they had the same ocean
here in Hawaii as we do in Los Angeles,
I would have floated here for free
instead of spending all that money
on plane tickets.

I'm Staring at Hawaii

There is a person parasailing
There are seven or eight sail boats
There is a row of solar panels on another building
There is another hotel's pool and their trees
There is the ocean
There are people on other balconies
There is a long way down from the sixteenth floor
There is a drop of water that came from the sky
There is the tip top corner of a Diamond Head
My feet may go there before this is all done

Aloha!

I forgot my belt in Newhall
so watch out Honolulu
you're about to get the
full Rick Lupert experience.

The Evening Shapes Up

Addie's not feeling well.
Jude is not of age.
I have no belt.
It's going to be a
Solo, pantsless trip
to get a Mai Tai tonight.

Influence

After a bottle
of pineapple sake
Addie's finger
enters my selfie.

If You're Going to Call Your Store *Cookies...*

There's a store called *Cookie's*
that only sells clothing.
I want to call them *liars*
until I see the cookie store
two doors down and figure
it's not worth it.

On the Lanai

It is colder than I imagine summer in Hawaii should be
on this balcony, or as my roommate Tony used to call them, *lanai*.

*A lanai is an indoor/outdoor roofed architectural feature
that has one "wall" open to the elements.* So why not!

Waikiki beach is below and empty....the fires have gone out
around the luau poles at the adjacent property.

It is hours later in my body than it is in my location.
We've already negotiated breakfast though I was

the only one with one eye open when it happened
so it could be a surprise to everyone when it happens.

The only belt for miles is an expensive one and
it doesn't seem worth it.

Two summers ago we were in Japan and now
we've barely traveled half that distance.

Though they were here once too.
We're about to find out all about it.

My Mistake

The fires haven't gone out.
The trade winds are just
diminishing their presence.
As the evening goes on
my presence, too,
diminishes.

Goodnight Waikiki

It is 10:30 in the evening in Hawaii
and I'm as tired as a school girl.

I may be mixing metaphors
but I'm not sure what I was going for

and this place seems to be a mix.
A mix of Los Angeles and Polynesia.

Of America and Japan.
Of ocean and pool.

The clock on my writing machine
has no intention of changing

and it reminds me of when I came from.
It is 10:30 in the evening in Hawaii

in Honolulu, in Waikiki, in this Village
and I'm going to sleep until...

well I'll let you know in the morning.

A Day
in Hawaii

It is seven in the morning in Honolulu, Hawaii.

If you had told me I'd be awake at seven
in the morning without any prompting from

electronics or a nudging hand, I would have
laughed you into the Pacific Ocean.

This is one of the effects of flying
the other way but not so far that you

cross the International Date Line.
I'm not sure if *International Date Line*

should be capitalized but it feels famous
enough to deserve it. The time we have

even at this early hour, is limiting our
breakfast options and we're prepared

for disappointment. Look how the uneven
lines on the right look like a wave

that someone is waiting to ride.
Poetry is water, is waves, is

a man teaching surf lessons after
feeding our Newhall cats.

There is a ship at the bottom of
the harbor. We will stand on top of it

today, and remember
how it got there.

Tourist

A comment online says
we should leave this Island
because it's a *tourist trap*.
Niagara Falls
The Eiffel Tower
The Grand Canyon
New York City
Pearl Harbor
Some of the most amazing places
attract so many people.
I embrace my *tourist* identity
as I get on a bus in the famous Waikiki
to be in the place where it happened.

You Had One Job

There's a crisis of faith happening
in our hotel room when we realize
the towel hooks in the bathroom
aren't sufficiently designed to
actually hold the towels.

Hands

Addie reaches for my hand in the tour bus
This is the kind of day she is having where
her fingers need to intertwine with mine.
This hand in mine, this is the kind of day
I'd like to have every day.

King David

was the last reigning king of Hawaii.
I guess this is where he went
after writing all those psalms.

On the Bus to the Sunken Boat

I
Our guide is so proud to tell us
that the Duke, whose statue we
are parked in front of, was good friends
With Shirley Temple. *Shirley Temple*
she says more slowly than other words.
She wants us to love her
as much as she thinks we should.

II
She keeps saying
hang on to your hats –
But it's not a metaphor.
It's windy and there's a
strong possibility our
hats will blow away.
(Alohat)

III
Don't eat the fish in the canal she says
just as we drive by a fishing local.

IV
The last queen of Hawaii
(Yes there was a queen)
lived in a condominium.
Autocorrect changed *lived* to
loved. I changed it back
but I hope she got to do that too.

V
The *Hawaii Five-0* theme is
playing in my head in front of the Ilikai Hotel.
This seems contextually appropriate
and also may be a brain condition.

VI
No one dies in the Waikiki Trolley.

VII
She says it's called *Hawaii Five-0*
because it's the fiftieth state.
I thought it was because *Five-0*
is code for police. This is a future
Jeopardy fist-fight in the making.

VIII
We drive by the world's
largest open air shopping mall.
And we keep on driving by.

IX
Gilligan left from the harbor to the left –
But our guide tells us they filmed
the rest of the show on the other side
of the Island. All those years shipwrecked –
all they had to do was walk over the mountain.

X
They burned down Honolulu Chinatown
to get rid of the rats. No rats died
so they imported mongoose to
eat the rats, but rats are nocturnal
and the mongoose slept through
all their opportunities to eat them.

XI
The Japanese are buying
a lot of Honolulu's land
which is a much nicer way
to go about it than
sending war planes.

XII
Honolulu –
protected bay

XIII
She emphasizes other words too
like *I know what they were doing
nine months earlier* after telling us
about the four hundred plus babies
born in one month at the Tripler
Army Medical Center.

XIV
The War of the Pacific
Tora tora tora
The ultimate surprise

XV
I ask Jude if he has his ticket
knowing full well I have it.
You have it he says
passing yet another test
that will allow him to progress
to the next level.

Pearl Harbor

Oil still leaks
from the USS Arizona

You can see the colored patches
floating on top of the water under

the memorial built over the smallest
fraction of the ship resting forever

on the harbor floor, the final resting place
for over a thousand men.

This is not an attraction
the park ranger tells us.

Yet so many people are attracted here
to see what was done after America

turned off the pipeline to Japan.
This sleeping giant awoke that day

and the price that was paid –
incalculable.

Post-Everything Fetish

The cemetery on Punch Bowl Crater is full.
So you cannot be buried there, unless you have
a loved one already there, in which case you
have the option to be buried on top of them
if that's your thing.

According To Our Guide

I
Mu'umu'u
is what you want
Not a mumu
(or moo moo)

II
The Hawaiian language only has
twelve letters. The most popular one is K.
This is why their words are longer and
by the time they tell you the name of
the street, you've already passed it.

III
King Kamehameha's favorite wife
was a large women which our guide
assures us was *super hot* for the day.

Addie asks if I'm her favorite wife.
*Of course you are honey...that's why
I never bring the others around.*

P.S. Just to be clear, there are no other wives.

Did We Choose The Right Vacation Destination?

Addie is concerned
the sand may be
sandy.

Aloha Shirts

They're called *Aloha shirts* and
not *Hawaiian shirts*. *Aloha* is not
as simple as *hello* or *goodbye*
or even *shalom* which is simply *peace*.
Aloha is a state of being you wish to achieve.
Your aloha is likely different from everyone else's.
This is why all the shirts are different.

Crazy Shirts

There is a store called *Crazy Shirts* where
I guess those shirts really get off the hook –
But it's closed so they're just sitting there
on their mannequins waiting for their cue
to begin the shenanigans.

I Miss a Sign That Says *High Curb*

So, sorry Joshua from Maryland
who's probably married by now
even though he's not when I'm writing this
and Rachel from Chicago
who probably has two babies by now
even though she only has one when I'm writing this.
I have nothing to say about that at this point.

I Am Not Writing a Book of Poems in Hawaii

Because this is a shorter trip
and Jude's along, I'm not
writing as much, I'm going to
have to use a much bigger font
so you get the size of book
you deserve.

P.S. This is not me admitting
to writing a book of poems
in Hawaii.

Hunka Hunka Hilton

Did I tell you this was Elvis Presley's
preferred hotel? There's a statue of him
and a detailed sign that tells you
this is where he stayed.

This is a nice full circle to our trip
to Memphis, two books ago, where
we went to his house which is
also where he stayed.

Like the full circle of being
in Pearl Harbor today where
our war began, after being in
Hiroshima, one book ago, where
our war ended.

Goodnight Honolulu

My eyes are so heavy right now.
Keeping them open is like a
separate visit to the fitness room.
I don't think I have the stamina for
any more poetry tonight.

A Second Day in Hawaii

On the Circle Tour

Duke is still getting leid today...

I
Jack assures us they no longer
practice human sacrifice.
Last week was the last one.

II
He tells us to be careful of the Pacific Ocean waves,
among the strongest in the world.
And also the naked old men who frequent the beach.

III
There's an unopened box of
Famous Amos cookies
in the rack above the seats
I wonder if these are in our future.

IV
And immediately, after writing number III
Jack announced we can have
snacks anytime we want
and breaks out a box of
assorted chip bags

V
Jack used to do slam poetry so
he's one of my people.

VI

He says Amos of the cookies
sold the company and now
sells pins at Waikiki and
he doesn't know why.

VII

The couple behind us
are from Wisconsin and
know of Oconomowoc
where we met.

VIII

We pass Bette Midler's house
I have no idea if she's home.

IX

The houses here are all five
to fifty million dollars and Jack
wants to make it convenient
for us and says we can simply
make checks out to him.

X

I assume we wait to use the bathroom
until we get back to the hotel tonight.
Jack confirms and points to the
plastic bag in the front of the bus.

XI

The blowhole at Cockroach Cove
is not the most impressive blowhole
but it's doing the best it can.

XII

When I get off the bus to use the bathroom
Jack says *get her done Ricky*
which is all the encouragement
I've ever needed.

XIII
Hawaiian comedians mostly
just attack other people's cultures
which, relatively speaking,
is a much nicer way to go about war.

XIV
Addie sees a horse off to the left
and says *horsey!* This is an
unpreventable, involuntary response –
kind of like when you see bubbles
and you're body automatically
forces you to say *bubbles!*

XV
We pass by a fire station but I assume
since we're in an island, when there
is a fire, they simply dip the burning
structure into the ocean.

XVI
You definitely don't want to
eat any food from that place
There is a reason they don't have a sign.
                              - Jack

XVII
I see Jack go into the bathroom
and tell him *get her done Jack.*
And now the circle is complete.

XVIII
We pay our respects
at a coconut graveyard.

XIX
Some of our group gets on the wrong bus.
That's how the *others* camp started.
And that, ladies and gentlemen,
is your *Lost* reference for today.

XX
A lot of people want to hold Jamaal's smoothie
while he goes to look for the missing people.
They're assuming they're never going to
see Jamaal again and don't want it to
go to waste.

XXI
Jack tells us we're going to the *marijuana*
he means *macadamia* nut farm but
tells us if we want the good stuff
head to the back of the store.

XXII
The notches where the cannons stood
are now just notches.

XXIII
Hawaii has the highest rate
of missing people. Their
Stairway to Heaven hike
is illegal.

XXIV
There are wild chickens
loose in the *Foodland* parking lot.
I'd like to open up the doors to
crazy shirts and let them
bock on in.

XXV
Jack is funny –
Legitimately standup funny.
I'm putting line breaks into his act
to turn it into my poetry.

XXVI

It's rainy and foggy on this side of the island.
We're heading to the macadamia nut farm
for nuts and coffee. Someone says there is
macadamia nut wine and Jack is ready to
jump off the wagon. Our son distracts
his story of lilikoi butter to point out the
shark shaped mailbox. Where was he?
Where are we?
Where are the nuts?

XXVII

There's talk of a farting competition
after lunch between Jack and Jude.
Let's go! They both say as they prepare
for their own Olympics.

XXVIII

Jack talks about his favorite scent
on earth. After telling us of his
skills in the farting competition
we know he's an expert.

XXIX

I just had *hella* free macadamia nut samples.

XXX

The idea for using blue crayons
to color water came from this
side of this island.

XXXI

More wild chickens.
Planet of the Apes would have
been a completely different movie
if it was wild chickens
instead of apes.

XXXII
Mother of the year
calls her kids while
she is in Hawaii.
Snippets of the conversation:
I'm gonna whoop you
I don't care that you're 19.
No souvenir for you.
Your sister gets
two souvenirs.

XXXIII
I stare out the bus window
eastward towards California.
I want to tell Addie I can see
our house. She won't take me
seriously; but then I'll clarify
in my mind. I can see our house
in my mind.

XXXIV
Jack tells us there are
fewer sharks at this beach
Which implies
still some sharks.

XXXV
Jack asks if we're ready for lunch.
Addie says she's *full of nuts.*
And now I have to hide this page
from her before this book is published.

XXXVI
The Shaka greeting (left finger and thumb)
developed when a man got his fingers
cut off in the sugar mill machinery.
That's how he waved to greet visitors.

XXXVII
The *secret beach*
by the shrimp farm
is frequented by nudists.

Addie wants to know if
it's the same naked guy at
both beaches.

Yes, I assume –
Traveling from beach to beach
through the local-only
nudist underground tunnels
(of love.)

XXXVIII
There are no tractors
at the shrimp farm.

XXXIX
I see what could be a wild ferret
and I want to bring it on the bus.
Addie tells me to be careful and
then regales me with tales of
her brother's ferret who would
take things like the remote control
and hide it under the couch, and
now I'm rethinking my whole plan
unless this wild ferret will agree
to not touch my stuff in exchange
for a lifetime supply of ferret food.

XL
Jack has this down
and it turns out this
is his company, so
he can stop where he wants
and say what he wants
no matter how off-color
without fear of a supervisor
saying things like
Jack, you shouldn't say that.
Jack has found his way
in this gathering place and
our seats in his bus have
brought us a few steps closer
to our aloha.

XLI
Is there anything to look at
Addie asks wanting to fill the space
between the end of our meal
and the return to the bus.
There's that fruit in that tree
I tell her pointing nearby
to a fruit I think we've never seen
with tourist names carved in
some of the leaves. Oooh
she says and heads in
that direction having been
provided with the perfect
Addie activity.

XLII
Sorry, secret nudists.
We've got sea turtles to meet.
You're on you own today.

XLIII
Jack gives out cookies
like it's the end of days
no consideration to his
bottom line.

XLIV
We've come to
the land of the
drowning coconut.

XLV
I suck on a suga cane
at Virgil's Farm stand
which brings me back to
the sugarcane plantation
in Louisiana. There is
so much this world
has in common.

XLVI
I chewed on a sugarcane today
sweet and grown on this soil.
I hear there's a lot of sugar in it
though.

XLVII
We drive by *Shark Cove*
which is filled with people
up to their waists in the water.
How lucky we are to be here at
feeding time.

XLVIII
(At Waimea Bay)
A wild chicken walks by
the ultimate saltwater aquarium
where the fish have never heard of glass
but know to stay away from my fingers.
I've got sand in every crevice but I
couldn't have been any more inside
the Pacific Ocean, the North Shore –
The waves carry me further and closer.
They'd carry me away if I let them.

XLIX
A lot of back and forth between Jack
and me and Addie leads to the phrase
ménage a turtle which was later refined
to *turtle a trois.*

L
We see sea turtles
which is confusing
when you say it
out loud.

LI
They pop their heads
out of the water
every thirty seconds
or so. A little more *or so*
than we'd prefer

LII
I could live
in a banyan tree
and be perfectly
happy.

LIII
Best shave ice
on planet:
Waiola
according to Jack.

LIV
Haleiwa is the name
of a little town that
we drive through, that
someday, I would like
to not drive through.

LV
Jack asks if we want to
stop at the coffee plantation
after the Dole plantation.
Yes, I say. *I speak for everyone*
I answer, taking control of
everyone's destiny.

LVI
Jude says he wants to go into
the maze at the Dole Plantation
thus inspiring the first *that's how*
we lost our last child of the vacation.

LVII
James Dole
of the pineapples
basically took Hawaii
by gunpoint
while King David
died in San Francisco.

LVIII
The Dole Plantation
coconuts and grilled corn station
is out of coconut.
End of days.
End of days.

LIX
The valley between
two mountain peaks
is where the Japanese
planes flew through
on their way to Honolulu.
A cross sits there now.

LX
Jack wants me and my insides
to know all about *Prima Yerba Blend*
pill cleanse.

LXI
Driving back – we pass an on ramp
to an *interstate* highway.
I forget which state or states
Hawaii is adjacent to.

LXII
Jack goes to Hooters
just for the breasts.
The chicken breasts
he clarifies.

At exactly six o'clock pm

at the corner of Ala Moana Blvd and Kālia Road
where the Hilton Hawaiian Village

juts into Waikiki's main thoroughfare
a man dressed in native hawaiian garb

runs out of the village with a stick of fire
and lights all the torches. For all I know

this has been going on since before
Elvis stayed here. Different guy, I'd suspect.

His buttocks, a little more visible than
one would expect in America.

Hawaii is its fiftieth and most recent state.
Some of the old ways are hard to let go of.

We walk by a shirt store called *Jimmy Choo*

I point to the sign and Addie says *Jimmy Choo*
to which I respond *geseundheit*
thus completing all of the plans
I had dreamed of for this moment.

Jack

I met Jack today
and so much of Oahu
Its hats and blowholes.

Its shrimp farms and
bird sanctuaries, its
macadamias and

just the heads of
its sea turtles.
The Pacific and I

became one.
I saw the valley
where the planes

first breached the land.
I had nuts and coffee
and sugarcane.

I had fruit,
the names of which
only my wife could remember.

I circled the island
with Jack who
told us everything he knew.

This was the day
that Jack Built.
Jack of the land.

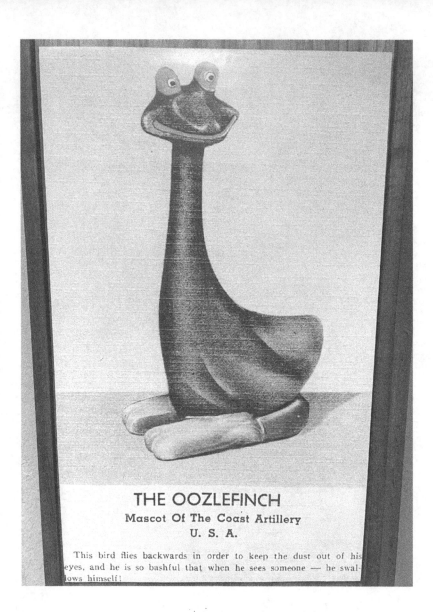

THE OOZLEFINCH
Mascot Of The Coast Artillery
U. S. A.

This bird flies backwards in order to keep the dust out of his
eyes, and he is so bashful that when he sees someone — he swal-
lows himself!

A Third Day in Hawaii

The Olympics Wake Me Up This Morning

The Olympics wake me up this morning
They came to my hotel room and
did gymnastics on the bed.

I don't know who gave them a key.
I recognized the announcer's voice
from when he was on the TV.

It was a thrill, to say the least.
Tickets are usually so hard to get.
Addie heard and rushed in.

She apologized for the commotion
(as if the Olympics are her fault.)
Jude stayed in the other room

clearing his throat. It was a little
early for me as I usually don't
have the Olympics over before coffee.

(And they didn't want any)
So I faced them towards the window
and went to take a shower.

Waiting for Breakfast
on Alo Moana Blvd.

I
They don't serve coffee at *Goofy Cafe and Dine*
to the people waiting for days and days to
have breakfast which is a crime against
alohumanity.

II
I am not the only one in this situation
The sun remembers my ankles
We are told not to block the door
    to the nail salon
The people at the tattoo parlor
    don't care
Coffee is a dream
A mask on my face
    imported from Twin Peaks
The white pigeon in the lanai
    wonders why we're doing this
And why we're not feeding her
(They call balconies *lanais* here.)
This is why people grab wild chickens
    off the sidewalk
    and have their way
Not us, of course
    That is not our way

III
Breakfast has mostly
been a disaster of poor
timing and long lines.

While waiting for breakfast

A man touched a leaf coming
out of a rain gutter.

The Olympics slept like babies.
People synced their devices.

I learned how to spell *synced*.
Sodas were delivered in bulk.

Coffee got uninvented.
The Roman Empire fell, again.

The bathroom key traveled the world.
People wrote their names on a list and prayed.

Babies were born
Some people chose not to have babies

not before coffee, anyway.

Waiting for Breakfast
During a Pandemic

A lady squeezes into the space next to me in the bench.
I scoot over a bit and she says *oh you're good.*
I'd be a lot better if you were wearing a mask, lady
in this space you just conquered. There's so much
I don't know about you before I feel good.

Fruit Wins

Addie asks me a question
but gets distracted while I answer
when a papaya walks by.
I know she loves me,
but where fruit is concerned
there is no competition.

I'm Still On This Whole *Lanai* Thing

Everyone has a different name for
the things that you can walk out on
outside your sliding glass door.
Hawaii has *lanais*.
New Orleans has *galleries*.
Some of us have *balconies*.
What do you call the thing you
walk out on so you can overlook
whatever you have to look over?

Actually At Breakfast

Our child has to stir the yogurt for days
in order for it to become appetizing to him.
Whatever it takes to get him through the day.

Long as She Can Grow It

Addie is proud of her wild
humid mane, growing like
a hundred pineapple in
the Hawaiian trade winds.

At the U.S. Army Museum

I
Jude wants to go to the army museum
to see the tanks and the helicopter
on the roof. I guess if it weren't for
the army we wouldn't be able to enjoy
Hawaii at all.
But at what price Pearl Harbor?
But at what price Hiroshima, Nagasaki?
But at what price aloha?

II
I see a multi colored
little tank I can only describe
as *cute*.

III
Addie suggests the
shark tooth club
would be a good one
to keep in our backpack.
(The smaller one)

IV
Kamehameha
secured his victory
on Oahu by
giving his enemy
(the natives
at the cliff)
the choice of
Jump or
be pushed.

They found the bones
when a tunnel for the freeway
was built by the descendants
of Dole.

V
War and *canoe*
are two words
that shouldn't
go together.

VI
All firearms in
this museum
are
inoperable.

Weapons everywhere
can learn from this.

VII
We haven't seen a good, empty
museum corner for me to walk into yet
so when the little nook leading to the
closed black iron door came along
it was time for my famous *walking
into something* photo!

VIII
The soldiers played *mule polo*
on their time off. Mules –
What can't they do?

IX
The Japanese will not go to war
with the United States. We are
too big. Too powerful. Too strong.
Vice Admiral William S, Pye
December 6, 1941

X
The Oozlefinch was the mascot of the
U.S. Army Coast Artillery Corps.

XI
Aquarius and *Let the Sunshine In*
greet us as we enter the army museum gift shop.
Even they are tired of war.
We buy an oozelfinch and head out
for shave ice.

Shave Ice

I
Big line at
Waiola Shave Ice
where Jack told us
to go.

II
Fire hydrant
in front of
Waiola shave ice
in case ice
burst into flames.

Walk to Hotel

I

Addie picks up ground flower
to put between her ear and her hair.
As if she needs anything to enhance
her beauty.

II

As we walk back to the hotel
from shave ice
our twelve year old sulks
because we are not taking a car
and we hear the Santa Clarita coyote
down the Honolulu street.
So much of these experiences
reminds me of home.

III

I can't tell if the young man
in the aloha shirt walking in front of us
is rapping or talking in the phone.

Or both!!

IV

We walk by a store called *Crazy Fish*
They are not wearing crazy shirts.

Bus Ride to the Nutridge Luau

Addie does the *hukilau*
while waiting for the bus
for the benefit of everyone on
Ala Moana Blvd.

Hohu, our driver
wants to get us in the mood.
The Hawaiian mood
he clarifies.

Hohu confirms Barack Obama
was born in America as we drive by
his elementary school. He also says
he knows this because he purchased
his birth certificate at a local ABC Store.

Round Top Drive will take us
on windy roads, through a forest
to the top of the hill. To Nutridge.

No one is happier than Jude
that the place is called *Nutridge*.

We go *up* the mountain
which goes against everything
Jane's Addiction taught me.

There are no predators in Hawaii –
No snakes, nothing but wild pigs.

At the Nutridge Luau

I miss the intro because I'm
already on the other side of the fence
in the bathroom.

The only rule is to
have a good time.

If we break the rule
we get a time out.

But their time out consists
of a million dollar view
and a beverage.

Lua means *bathroom.*
Luau means *party.*
It's different.

We're on the youngest land
on the island

They keep growing the *king's crop*
of sweet potato.

This is where chocolate covered
macadamia nuts come from.
Not just this island, but this farm.

We're going to get our kid a *virgin.*
Context is everything.

Flower in the left ear *taken*
Flower in the right *available*
Flower in both *confused*

David keeps pulling fruits and
nuts out of his pocket

Are those huge avocados
in his pocket or is he just...
...Family show, family show.

Jude isn't so good with the spear throwing.
The guide tells us not to worry.
Gatherers are important too.

The rock game
is, suspiciously, a lot like
people throwing rocks
at each other.

The bigger the flower
The more desirable you are.
Addie's blocks out the sun.
I get a dilapidated petal situation
with a lone stamen reaching for eternity.

We see the burn marks
on the hands and feet of
the fire dancer.
This is not a drill.

For some reason the whole experience
ends with *YMCA* and the *Electric Slide*

On the way home
Hohu wants us to raise our hands
if we're not here.

Nutridge

Historic home
Gable and Presley's feet
touched its soil.

First with running water.
Newest land on the land.
The gathering place

of gathering places.
Jokes and disco.
Fire and hula.

The casual spirit.
More food than
we ever needed.

They'll send you home
with a box of pineapples
if you want.

Speaking of home –
We don't have to go home –
but we can't stay here.

Though we'd like to.

Last Dance

Addie and I dance
as close as possible to

*I Can't Help Falling
in Love With You.*

Elvis stayed here so,
it all makes sense.

*Take my hand
Take my whole life too*

I gave her both
She reciprocated

We couldn't help it.

A Fourth Day in Hawaii

I remember being in the ocean two days ago.

The temperature of the water
and my body were the same.

I flowed with the waves until
I became water.

The fish started to trust me.
I hear there were even positive words

in the sea turtle community.
I forgot who and what I was that hour.

But my red ankles, two days later
will not let me forget, I was there.

Day Trip

Today we will visit the islands of Polynesia without ever leaving Oahu. Ask me about the magic that makes this possible!

Addie hasn't found anything she likes at Starbucks

which has humiliated everyone in Seattle
where corporate headquarters set up

an *Addie Department* to develop new beverages
just for her. They release one into the

global network and monitor. It may be
weeks or months before she stops in

discovers it and gives it a try.
This one's too sweet she'll say out loud

(which is the best way to say things)
and the whole department will weep, defeated

then take a week off to recover. Then back to it
hoping to win her over. *Why are we at Starbucks*

in Hawaii you may ask. Because we had a *second*
to get to the bus to all of Polynesia and

it was right there, impossibly convenient
marked up with Island resort gusto

and ready to try and try again.

It is humid today

is a sentence that could
begin every day.

It doesn't matter
how showered I am

how clean my clothes –
a half a morning

in this inclement
and it's like I've been

shipwrecked
for eternity.

It is humid today

The trade winds
come early and
save the day.

Bag Addie

Addie wants to buy a bag
Not a temporary bag but
a permanent one.

I want to be there
when the bag is paid for –
physically hand the card.

The act of giving a gift
that she picks out
part of our forever love.

Lexa

The woman who sells us the bag
tells us her sister has sixty nine letters
in her Hawaiian first name.
Dude.

Bus Ride to Polynesia

I
We'll have to give up
these front row bus seats
if a handicapped comes.
Since I bumped my head
on the screen getting into
the seat, I think I now qualify.

II
There's a canoe pageant
in our near future.

I hope it's *peace* canoes
and not one of those war canoes
we saw at the army museum.

III
We wear masks and
they take our temperatures
before getting in the bus.
The price of pandemic paradise.

IV
We pass by a thin hotel
whose lanais point towards the
mountains instead of the ocean
a punishment given by the fat hotels
who've long since outgrown the
hotel shaped bikinis of their youth.

V
We pass by a noticeably thin hotel.
The other hotels have grown fat
with tourists and lilikoi butter.

VI
The things Addie pulls
out of her purse –
CVS has nothing on her.

VII
Addie says if more than half the poems
mention her, it's not okay. I try to distract her
with a nearby lizard fence so I can
discretely write this down.

VIII
We pass by *Hawaiian Rent-All*.
I'm quickly asked to leave after
presenting my list of items they
do not have to rent.

IX
In another part of the island
near *Chinaman's Hat*
are two sharp mountain peaks
pointing to the sky which I'm
reminded to not refer to as
Chinaman's Tits.

X
We drive by *Likelike Highway*
and Addie wants to know
what if you don't like it?

XI
We drive through *Haiku*
Cross *Haiku Road.* May not mean
what I think it means.

XII
Depending on what you do
with your fingers, you could be
praising satan, flipping someone off
or Hawaiian chakra hanging loose.
So pay attention to your digits,
my friends. It could change everything.

XIII
The driver to the
Polynesian Cultural Center
does not speak at all.
This is not a tour.
It is merely a ride.

XIV
I send Brendan a picture of Addie
with the pineapple from last night's farm.
He reminds me to tell her how beautiful she is –
That she takes his breath away.
What he said, I tell her pointing at the phone
and then we kiss through masks
imported from Seattle.

XV
Cover of the Hawaii Five 0 Theme
(abridged)

Ba ba ba ba ba ba
Ba ba ba ba ba ba
Ba ba ba ba ba ba
Ba ba ba ba ba ba

XVI
I want to adopt a highway
but I wouldn't know what to feed it.

XVII
A caution sign warns of
children see-sawing.
It feels like planning mistakes
were made in either the
location of the see-saw
or the location of the road.

XVIII
Another caution sign says
Rumble Strip.
Aww it's about to go down!

XIX
A house on stilts with
only a ladder going up to the door.
That's not how I want to live.

At the Polynesian Cultural Center

I
Only the chief enter the Fiji hut
from the western door unless
you want to get clubbed to death.
(We do not.)

II
Breadfruit or *umu*
is the second most popular starch
in the Polynesian islands.
But I hear the scoring is
very political.

III
It's almost impossible
for someone to be allergic to poi.
But we're sure going to try!

IV
We try poi
on the Hawaiian island
I make sure to take a poicture.

V
Learn all the island greeting words.
There will be a test at dinner.
If you pass, you get to have dinner.
If you fail, you become dinner.

VI
All of these Fijian warriors
reenacting a battle in traditional garb –
Everyone of them, in real life,
has an email address.

VII
I tell Jude that last Fijian dance is what
we had in mind for his Bar Mitzvah.
He's all for it when we tell him about
the club he gets to use on an attendee.

VIII
In Fiji the coconut tree
is the tree of life.

Each coconut
Has a unique face.

He majors in business finance
but minors in coconuts.

IX
The Luperts trade in their Japanese vehicles
for Tongan canoes. Emergency exits to the right
and left. Powered by the arms we brought with us.

X
The water at the Polynesian cultural center
is only two feet deep. So if you find you are drowning
just stand up.

XI
Our canoe approaches.

XII
I want to declare war on another canoe.
I want to declare peace on another canoe.

XIII
Addie is quite proud of her unique talent:
being able to scrape an entire coconut of its meat.

Jude has us covered with
eating large amounts of *Chex Mix*.

I'm pretty good at documenting it all.

XIV
Tahitian Wedding

The hat of the guy at the Tahitian wedding
seems too big to be safe.

The groom's hat is even taller
and almost takes down a wire holding up a plant.

The woman who gave us the coconut bread
is also the bride – On her wedding day!

We get to renew our vows, Tahitian style!
Finally, Jude gets to be at our wedding.

XV
We enter the *Ukulele Experience* at the exit
and learn how a finished ukulele
is turned into a tree.

XVI
Elvis filmed several scenes of
Paradise, Hawaiian Style here.
We can't go anywhere without
stepping in Elvis' footsteps.

XVII
We take an ukulele lesson
or more realistically,
Jude takes an ukulele lesson
and Addie and I play chords
like bosses.

XVIII
The driver back asks us if
anyone left any children in the center.
Just drive I scream in a panic
but then realize Jude is already
on the bus.

(Just kidding Jude)

Easy As

On Kalakaua Ave., there's an ABC Store next to a 123 Store. It's no longer in vogue to make Michael Jackson references so we'll just have to ignore this perfect storm of geographia.

Hawaiiku

Satisfying cheese
plate at *Island Vintage Wine
Bar*. My mouth thanks you.

My Tai

We're sitting at the Mai Tai Bar
at the beach at The Royal Hawaiian.
Our twelve year old doesn't seem

interested in the ocean since
*I don't have my phone to take
pictures of it.*

I tell him there's nothing like the
natural beauty of the world...
outside of your mother's eyes.

I try to contain myself but burst out
laughing after the suspicious look in
Addie's eyes unravels my composure.

Jude wants me to explain what I
just said and I try but I think I just
lose him more so I say *here's an umbrella, kid*

handing him the one that came with
their *Signature Mai Tai* which
brought us to this place, long after

either of them wanted anything to do
with food or drink...they just wanted
to make me happy. And as the drink

goes into my mouth, like so many others
in so many cities and countries have
I truly am.

I Don't Remember
The First Two

I got a third dent
and it's in my leg
Jude shouts
halfway through my
Mai Tai.

Plan

Brunch
Hike
Lagoon
Poke

The plan for tomorrow
has been decided.

One Period at End of Poem

I've got Mai Tai on the brain
and throughout my blood
And it's late
And everyone wants an Uber
And I want to walk
And there's the ocean
And it's dark
And the bed may not come
for a thousand years.

Boo

The guy smoking on the beach
next to my Mai Tai experience
is ruining my entire Hawaii.

And also

the crazy fish store
sells clothing
and not fish
of any kind.

A Fifth Day in Hawaii

Brunch Line

I
It is August today and
there are twenty-one parties
ahead of us, so we have
entered a backup line
and hope to have brunch
sometime before we
leave the island.

II
I experience my own Pearl Harbor
waiting in the brunch line when
the woman behind me starts
flailing her hat around to pass the time
and it enters my air space.

III
A woman fills the
hand sanitizer station with
Healthy Premiere Pro hand sanitizer.
So at least there's that.

Music To My Ears

Israel Kamakawiwo'ole sings
Henehene Kou'Aka to us
over these sticky breakfast tables.

Our waiter, Jaime, who has had
enough of our questions, says
he will turn it down. This is not necessary

for my ears which have longed
to be serenaded by Israel Kamakawiwo'ole
since I first heard he existed a few days ago.

Are There Too Many of Us?

A *Google News* notification tells us
The Hawaiian Tourism Authority
has approved a plan to *reduce tourists*.
I hope it doesn't happen while we're here
Or, if it does, we don't get culled.

More Israel

A bird comes to visit Addie
while we wait for the check.
And the song comes on again
probably five times now.
The island shuffle.

Manoa Falls

I
We drive through the punch bowl
to the hike. I feel my presence
is spiking the punch.

II
Jude says the trees are wearing clothes
which is more than I can say about my
morning walk from the shower to the balcony.
Waikiki!

III
At the head of the trail I ask
a family finishing their hike
if it was worth it.

I was hoping they'd say *no*
so I could say *forget it* then
turn around back to the rideshare spot
a few yards away for comedy effect.
It didn't work out that way.

IV
A shipping container becomes a bridge,
and every tenth hiker gets transported to China.

V
I want to see the tree where
Charlie hung himself in *Lost*.
Not because I'm macabre but
because I'm a fan of the show
and I like to be where things happened.

VI
Manoa falls trickles from
the top of the mountain
to the pool below
where people swim
not far past the sign that says
Do not go beyond this sign.

VII
So many cell phones
up and down the trail
including the one I'm
writing this book on.

VIII
It's thin but it's pretty
Addie says, which is
what she must see
every time she
looks in a mirror.

IX
Want to see where this one goes
I ask pointing to a new trailhead which
Leads to a lookout a mere 1.7 additional
miles away. Jude says *no*
before I can even finish the question.

X
It's advised to
let gravity do the work
on the way down
so I stand completely still
and nothing happens so
I have to walk the rest of the way
under my own power.

XI
A lot of people carrying
babies up and down the trail.
Lazy, lazy babies.

XII
I keep posing long after the picture has been taken...
Addie takes her time telling me I can stop now.

XIII
Jude says he's peeing now
so he won't have to do it later.
Ahh Jude, my little fruit fly –
You have a lifetime of peeing
ahead of you.

XIV
We just saw a chicken cross the road
I'm sad to report it would not
explain why.

XV
You could save a lot of waterfall effort
with a few rocks and a well placed hose.

Bad Uber Driver

We learn about the Uber scam
where the driver makes a quick five dollars
if they tell you they have an emergency and
cancel your ride. Fascinating. I wish
this didn't happen at a trail head
on the remote edge of town
forcing us to wait another twenty minutes
for a more ethical driver.
We refused to cancel and then
received an email from Uber telling us
the driver cancelled saying we weren't wearing masks.
Oh, Uber customer support, prepare for the
Rick Lupert onslaught that is about to
head your away. This is less of a poem
and more of an infomercial. Sorry,
you don't have to buy anything.

Ocean, Lagoon, Pool

I
In the Pacific Ocean
the waves and I develop a relationship
One based on trust and symmetry

II
I use my fancy voice
normally reserved for fine dining
to announce each wave.

III
Addie is proud of me
when I announce I can stand up
and do so.

IV
Diamond Head is out today
occasionally a cloud makes
its presence known.

V
Jude has sand in places
that don't exist.

VI
A ship comes in
The Atlantis, it's called.
Addie asks *what's that?*
A ship I say.

VII
They head to the lagoon
and shave ice.
I head to the super pool
which is the same temperature as me.

VIII
Finding chairs at the *Super Pool* –
One must embrace their inner vulture.
Eventually I swoop in and
take my pray –
My comfy pray.

IX
Then comes the part where
everyone and their young son
wants to know if I need
all three of these chairs.

X
The *Super Pool*
is a lot of bigger people
lifting and throwing
smaller people.

XI
I sit under a tree
that's had its
head cut off.

XII
Everyone in my family
tells me how horrible
the shave ice was.

XIII
Jude asks if I want
to *try* a Funyun.
I assure him I've lived
a lifetime full of snack foods
before he came along.

Waikiki!

Addie has her own *Waikiki* moment unintentionally on the lanai.

Poke

I
Jude and I are both wearing red shirts
on the way to *Redfish Poke* and we're
wondering if they'll give us a discount.

P.S. Quick followup: They will not.

II
Our interactive waitress
asked a lot of questions
and provided more answers
than we could possibly ever need.

Short answer: *No.*

Jude says

I have a leaf in my pocket 'for later.'
We demand context
and he tells us he wants to
throw it out our hotel window
Later he tells us he also
has a rock from the beach –
But he won't tell us what it's for.

A Short History of Hawaii

There was a king and
he made many men
jump off a cliff

and thus the
Hawaiian islands
were united.

Later King David
(Not of the Jews)
died in San Francisco.

His sister took over
but the rich man who
invented pineapples

used his guns to
give Hawaii to America.
Now there are

statues of surfers
and all of the Americans
from the mainland

are lined up
to eat brunch
in Waikiki.

Are You Reading This?

I'm not sure if the cloud is working
and I may have lost some poems.
If you see any of my poems in your cloud
please send them to me on a rainbow.
There's a shiny macadamia nut in it for you.
They call them *mac nut* here.
But you can call them what you like.

We finish the evening with ice cream.

It is our last night in this town
before we make the short Hawaiian journey to Kapolei

home of Aulani, and we assume, more lines.
But these will be *Disney lines* and

no one does lines better than them.
We're not sure the fish will sing

like in the commercial
but there will be music and money spent

and food eaten. We do these things at home too
but they come with other responsibilities.

On this Island, all we have to do is
get in the ocean and wait for a fish to sing.

A Sixth Day in Hawaii

Wild Kingdom

I discover Addie's feet jiggling in the bed.
I'm not sure what's happening, but it is
truly amazing when you introduce a
biological entity to a new habitat.

We are leaving Waikiki today

but not before French toast
at the place with *heaven* in its name
and not before taking a photo with
Shirley Temple's bronze friend
and not before *Surfboard Alley*
and not before we give its sun one last chance
       to apply its color
and not before coffee flown in from another island
and not before we buy something with a turtle on it
and not before we wonder how climate change will affect all of this
and not before we shake the sand out of our water shoes
and not before we take the shirts off the hangers
and not before we brush our teeth
and not before one last everything.

Waikiki!

I do a final nude walk from
the bathroom to the view
but am intercepted by Addie
who is thrilled that I'm clean.

Hawaiiku

We coat ourselves with
the oils of our day and
walk into the sun.

This

If I lived in Honolulu
I'd be home now.

At Heavenly Island Lifestyle

They let Addie sub soup for the taro muffin
and I wonder what other substitutions are possible?
Instead of lemonade, can I have a new car?
Instead of silverware, can it be a forest?
Instead of coffee, could I get all the sand they imported from Australia?
Instead of vegetables, would it be possible to get bigger vegetables?
Instead of the French toast I ordered, could I get
the keys to your house and a map to your treasures?
I'll take the coffee as is.

Aloha

If you drink enough of your coffee
you're rewarded with the word *aloha*
printed on the inside of the mug.
This was not a problem for me but
I have a feeling they would have
given me an aloha no matter
what I ordered.

At One Point Addie is Replaced by a Bird

At one point I look up and
instead of Addie there is a bird

sitting on the pillow where I last saw her.
I'd always thought this might happen.

Thankfully there are no HOA prohibitions
about birds back at home.

I don't know if this bird looks hungry
and I know for a fact Addie just ate.

On Waikiki Beach

Jude proposes to a pigeon.
This should make the rehearsal dinner easy
(If she says yes.)

This Is Not Where We Will Dine Tonight

Stopping in a Subway feels like
a crime against humanity in Hawaii
but the boy's hungry and it can't be
all about me and my fancy desires.

Waikiki

If you were the ocean
you would wash up here too.

Hawaii Five-0 Theme Reprise at Waikiki Beach

Ba ba ba ba ba ba
Ba ba ba ba ba ba
Ba ba ba ba ba ba
Ba ba ba ba ba ba

Paueli, our driver to Aulani

has three kids, the oldest nineteen.
He doesn't look older than nineteen himself.
This is part of the magic of the Island.

Outside of this car he deals with *anything paint*.
We compare prices on whole house jobs
since we recently acquired a whole house.

We complain about love letters from
home owners associations containing
demands and fines. *Your mailbox*

is the wrong color. *Your trim is fading.*
It's out of control. He takes us on the *interstate*
away from the city of the city Island.

You can always escape. His daughters
track him around the island and occasionally
get impatient and demand *Cash App* tributes.

He shows us the mountain where he lives
and says we are going to the other side.
His friends want him to sell his house.

They say *sell your house Paueli.*
Then buy two. Rent one, and live in the other.
His daughters won't allow it. They're too happy.

Our trip on the *interstate* is a convenience for him.
Paueli will be looking down on us from his mountain tonight.
His daughter's lullabies carried to us on the trade winds.

Aulani

We check in to *Aulani, a Disney Resort*
having mortgaged our house to be able to afford it.
There are bird sounds coming out of the TV
as one would expect.

There is a lazy river right outside the room
the closeness of which should partner well
with my laziness.

No Singing Fish

The commercials promised us
the fish would sing at Aulani.
They did not but there are fish
and they are beautiful, as is
everywhere here. How lucky we are
to be able to be here with the
manufactured magic we so adore.

Down the Volcanic Vertical Slide

Like a water *Space Mountain*
housed in a Hawaiian
Big Thunder Mountain.

Quiet, Sherman Oaks Man!

A man on his phone to
Sherman Oaks, talks so loud
they could hear him in Sherman Oaks
without his phone.

Tradition!

Jude tries to convince us
it's a tradition to keep four
ketchup packets from dinner
in the hotel fridge. I don't
remember this one from
Hebrew school but maybe
he's Reform.

At The Olelo Room

One of them plays a left handed
twelve-string guitar

the other, a stand up bass.
They're *standing up*

behind plexiglass screens
as is the custom of our time.

For a Hawaiian duo they play a lot of
classic English tunes.

We learn that's because that's what
table thirty-three wants.

But we here in *table back of the room*
want to hear more Israel Kamakawiwo'ole.

Our waiter says the song we *Shazamed*
is one of his favorites. Ours too now.

They play something Hawaiian with
a strumming that you have no choice

but to internalize. They play
I Can't Help Falling in Love With You,

again, and I can't help but weep.
Addie's drink is too sweet

which she communicates by moving
her lips back and forth in a way that

I didn't know was possible.
All we needed was that last song.

It's 10:00 which might as well be
a million o'clock the way we feel

Our sleeping child in another room
beckons.

A Seventh Day
in Hawaii

Ohana

Every morning at seven o'clock
the Ohana woman chants us awake.
Her voice also sent us back to our room

at eleven o'clock in the evening.
I think she goes with the tiny lights
that appear in the sidewalk at night

but only sometimes, so seeing them
and especially photographing them
is not a sure thing.

Today is our last day on the Island
except for the part of the day
we will be here tomorrow.

I have two more chances to
document her voice and add it
to the soundtrack of this trip.

Soundtrack of this trip is not a metaphor.
I am recording not just with these words, but digitally
and will be able to *play* Hawaii whenever I feel like it.

I feel like the Ohana woman will only be available
in my ears here. She is not a character but
the voice of this place.

We have a full day of not leaving this place
ahead of us today. Plates will clink.
Water will touch every part of us.

It will rain in full view of the sun.
Fish will take their meals.
We will see fire tossed and twirled.

We will have leis placed around our necks
one last time. Then we will hear her voice
one last time.

Uncle tells stories a couple of times a day.

They just call him *Uncle* without any
possessive word like "my" or "our."
Like how they refer to *Big Island*
as *Big Island* without the *the*
I so desperately want to hear.

Nose Hair May Save Your Life

I see an article suggesting nose hair
may help in preventing viruses like
the common cold, and now I think
the nose hair trimming attachment
on my personal grooming kit may
have been lying to me this whole time.

Addie tells Jude

to put the waffles on top of the potatoes so
they don't get frosting on them.
This is the kind of pro leftovers packing tip
one can expect when traveling with her.

Hawaiiku

Three cups of coffee
did it for me. I'm moving
like Ginger Rogers.

Free Back Scratcher

I got a free back scratcher last night
after ordering the *Tropical Itch Cocktail*
at the The Olelo Room. After leaving, and
possibly influenced by the rum and bourbon
I told every one we walked by, strangers
in the Aulani dark, *I got a free back scratcher*
and held it up for them to see. Also I
accidentally left the back scratcher in the bar
and Addie noticed and said *your back scratcher?!*
and I said *oh no!* and ran all the way back to the bar
where it was waiting for me on the still uncleaned table.
Jude said, later, *that's a nice back scratcher*
which made me feel awfully good about
his upbringing.

Lazy River

I
I let Jude do
all the work
in the lazy river
because
lazy river.

II
We pass several
empty tubes in
the lazy river.
Some people
didn't make it.

III
I want to take
the lazy river
back to California.
But, not today.

Later, Down the Volcanic Vertical Slide

I heartily laugh while sliding which is
broadcast to the people waiting at the bottom
like I just invented radio. *So you heard me*
I ask Jude. *We all heard you* says a stranger
Ahh good I say. *There's no extra charge for that*
It comes with the resort fee.

By The Pool

I
Jude's doing a toe count
of every bird he sees
since he saw one missing
four of them. *Oh good*
this one has all its toes
I hear him saying before
I drift off with the trade winds.

II
Pacific Ocean Lagoon.
Lazy river.
Poolside drink.
Not life goals –
Life accomplishments.

III
Any experience not involving
drinking a coconut mint mojito
next to a pool, next to an ocean
can suck it.

IV
A topless sea captain walks by.
I can tell he's a sea captain
because of his sea captain hat.

V
I wear a long sleeve black *scorcher*
partially to protect me from the sun
and partially so people don't know what
a Sasquatch disaster I've become.

VI
This book doesn't have a lot of
observations about art in museums
as much of what we did was outside.
But if you're looking for ekphrastic observations
may I recommend that you purchase
every one of my previous books
that are chock full of them?

VII
Cancel everything else
but this.

VIII
I want to take a bath in goldfish
Jude says, and I lift up the rim of my hat
because I didn't hear him and he says it again
I want to take a bath in goldfish
at which point I put the rim of my hat back down
as I don't need to hear any more.

IX
You can get Mickey ear shaped shave ice here
but when it starts to melt it's kind of a
rainbow colored horror show.

X
Addie comes back super relaxed
from her massage where another man
touched her all over with sticks, stones
and his hands. It was my idea actually.
We're in island mode and when she asks me
what I want to do, I take a hundred years to answer.

XI
The notification that it's time to check in
for our flight home tomorrow arrives like an insult.
No, I will never leave this place and its
poolside drinks, and its Pacific Ocean
gently lapping up against the imported sand.
It's time to check in to a long nap
followed by a luau. I'm getting leid tonight
American Airlines. Don't bother me.

Waiting in Line for the Luau

I get nervous with open seating
since everyone and their uncle
are taller than me.

I'm in the line early.
Early enough to be in the front
But not VIP enough to be in the preferred.

All the people behind me
are eying the tables like people
searching for beach chairs at the Hilton.

This is almost it for Hawaii
So this could make or break it
This last taste in our mouths

If Mickey doesn't
make an appearance
there'll be hell to pay.

I'm standing next to the founder stones

which is where I think I'm supposed to stand.
Though there is no sign or cast telling us.
Everyone behind me is trusting that
I have stopped in the right spot.
This is the power I wield over these people
from all over the world. I could probably
charge them a fee for something solely on
the auspices of where I am standing.
By the Founder's Stones
where the Knox family
from Benton, Maine
have their name
on a tile
on a stone.

At This Luau

I
I wonder if the
Moana Surprise dessert
is Moana jumping out of
a shave ice.

II
Addie wants to know
what the *Virgin Hula Girl*
drink is.

III
It is pleasing to eat.

IV
They've been calling us *Ohana –*
family since we arrived
I'm starting to believe it.
Alooooooha.

V
An American Airlines plane
flies over the luau.
What a terrible reminder.

VI
We string flowers together
for our wrists and necks.
This is all Addie ever wanted.

VII
Jude and I double dog dare each other
during a break from the performances
to go up to one of the empty platforms
and do interpretive dances.
He refuses but is so ready with the camera
for me to make my move.

VIII
You must always
arrive to a luau
with a heart filled with
aloha.

IX
Hawaiiku

All the world's people
should gather at a luau
forget their conflicts.

X
Can't talk –
Mickey and Minnie
just showed up to the luau.

XI
It is a privilege to care for
and enjoy the bounty of this land.

XII
The mighty sub
The leaping fish of water
The guardian shark
The water lizard
And the love of this land

XIII
Aloha is wrong and true
Aloha is something
that will last you a lifetime.

XIV
He takes fire with his hand
from one end of the stick
and moves it to the other.
With his bare hand.

XV
We are now all
a part of this together.

Aulani Sky

This star I am staring at
when normally I can't see
any stars –

How long did this light
take to get to my eye
and is someone there

staring back?

Kahala

We meet Kahala at the front desk
who tells us about the chant that
happens at seven and eleven.

The first secret – it also happens at noon
announcing the important times of day.
My plan is to walk out onto our balcony

at eleven in this evening and
receive this chant with my ears,
heart and audio recorder.

The words are different
depending on what time of day it is.
You begin the day, you mark time

in the middle of the day, and
you end the day. We are ending the day
we do not want to end.

Kahala has two babies inside her
and knows everything she needs to know
to tell them when they come out –

The meanings of the chants.
The history of the feathered instrument.
The fact that it is called an *'uli'uli.*

She knows where to buy one and
uses phrases like *where I buy my hula supplies.*
She wants us to send her pictures

of mainland children with 'uli'ulis.
There is nothing but music on this Island.
Music and family.

Practical

Addie practices opening and closing the barn door
leading to the bathroom from the hotel bedroom.
Since we're getting one of these back home
she wants to be prepared.

We Leave Ohana
for Home

Seven A.M.

I
Sure enough
at seven a.m.
the ohana woman
chanted us awake.

II
At seven a.m.
there are already people
in the lazy river which
defeats the whole purpose.

Aloha

A shuttle is coming, today
to take us away.

I can't decide whether
I should give them the evil eye

or continue on
with the aloha spirit.

"Disney is not in the discount business"

We received our bill
for Disney's Aulani.
We're going to have to
sell Jude to pay for it.

Hawaiiku

Big eyed Mickey lamp –
surfboard, ukulele. Switch –
other side of room.

Forecast

Smooth skinned pale people
getting off planes in Honolulu.
Red peeling skin monsters
getting on.

Potato Truth

Jude announces
this is my last potato
but then has another.

This is like yesterday
when he said *you can have
the rest of the fries*

but then continued to eat them.
You can't trust this kid
when it comes to potatoes.

Jude is Bird Happy

Look at all the birds on that roof.
What happened to all the toes on this one.
I recognize this one from yesterday.
I'm going to call this one Stuart.

found

For you is
this adornment.
It is told through
everlasting love.
Wear this lei –
It's for you, the one
who had come.

An hour before the shuttle takes us away

Mickey and Minnie are downstairs at the bar
not drinking but posing for photos on
the band's stage. This aloha has taken
it all out of me so I stay on the couch
in the lobby upstairs. This is the longest
denouement in poetry history.

I Think It Was Waimea Bay

A woman at *Hale Moana* gift shop
asks if I know the name of the beach
we went to. I know it was in the North Shore
but without scrolling up a lot, the best I can do
is humiliate myself by letting all twelve
Hawaiian letter spill out of my mouth
and hope it's somewhere near
the answer she is looking for.

I'll be Ready

I receive a voice mail saying
my appointment on the twenty-first is confirmed
But I'm not sure what it's for.
The real world can be so vague.

It is *Now*, Everywhere

I'd like to look at the ocean
one last time before we go
but I'm afraid it will make me weep.

You may say it is the same ocean
I have in my back yard, but
the ocean is always bluer

on the other side.
The ohana woman chants again
at eleven-thirty heralding

the middle of the day. She will
do this again tonight at eleven
and tomorrow morning at seven

and so on, every day, forever
wherever I am on Earth
even after I have become dust.

Ka Momi O Ka Pakipika

The song from the fish commercial
that brought us here plays again
in the lobby. I *Shazam* it and can now
make Aulani anywhere I go.

Airport Shuttle

I
The driver asks if we're ready to go home.
We say *no* in unison, like we've
been rehearsing this our whole lives
and further ask her to drive slow.

II
We don't get to sit in the front row
on the shuttle bus. Already the world
is crashing down around us.

III
I misread the sign that says
Hawaiian Self Storage as
Hawaiian Surf Storage.

IV
The next sign definitely says
Aloha Bus Stop.

V
A van definitely has
Aloha Junk Man
stenciled on it.

VI
I wonder if they have
a fitness center at the airport
or if I should plan on
wandering onto the tarmac
and lifting airplanes
over my head.

VII
We are on the *interstate* again.
Ha ha ha ha ha ha!

VIII
Taking us to the airport
after a vacation should be
considered a crime.

IX
I see the aloha electric grid
taking aloha energy
to the aloha family.

At the Airport

I see a book called
The Big Island Revealed.
Put yours pants on Big Island!

On the Plane

Addie pulls out eleven neatly packaged bags of snacks
including dried fruit, macadamia nuts, gluten free pretzels,
a granola bar, a handful of things I can't identify
and so much more from God-knows-where in her backpack
lays them across her seat back table, stares at the feast
of options she has transported almost twice across the ocean
and says *slim pickins* at which point I'm not sure
I'll be able to take her seriously again.

Everyone

in Hawaii
thinks
Los Angeles
is
close.

I wish

this
wasn't the
last poem
in
this book.

Rick Lupert will return in
The Low Country Shvitz.

The author hiding behind a bamboo stalk.

Three-time Pushcart Prize, and Best of the Net nominee Rick Lupert has been involved with poetry in Los Angeles since 1990. He was awarded the Beyond Baroque Distinguished Service Award in 2014 for service to the Los Angeles poetry community. He served for two years as a co-director of the non-profit literary organization Valley Contemporary Poets. His poetry has appeared in numerous magazines and literary journals, including *The Los Angeles Times, Rattle, Chiron Review, Red Fez, Zuzu's Petals, Stirring, The Bicycle Review, Caffeine Magazine, Blue Satellite* and others. He edited the anthologies *A Poet's Siddur: Shabbat Evening - Liturgy Through the Eyes of Poets, Ekphrastia Gone Wild - Poems Inspired by Art, A Poet's Haggadah: Passover through the Eyes of Poets,* and *The Night Goes on All Night - Noir Inspired Poetry,* and is the author of twenty-five other books: *The Tokyo-Van Nuys Express, Hunka Hunka Howdee!, 17 Holy Syllables, God Wrestler: A Poem for Every Torah Portion,* (Ain't Got No Press) *Beautiful Mistakes, Donut Famine, Romancing the Blarney Stone, Professor Clown on Parade, Making Love to the 50 Ft. Woman, The Gettysburg Undress* (Rothco Press), *Nothing in New England is New, Death of a Mauve Bat, Sinzibuckwud!, We Put Things In Our Mouths, Paris: It's The Cheese, I Am My Own Orange County, Mowing Fargo, I'm a Jew. Are You?, Feeding Holy Cats, Stolen Mummies, I'd Like to Bake Your Goods, A Man With No Teeth Serves Us Breakfast* (Ain't Got No Press), *Lizard King of the Laundromat, Brendan Constantine is My Kind of Town* (Inevitable Press) and *Up Liberty's Skirt* (Cassowary Press), and the spoken word album *Rick Lupert Live and Dead* (Ain't Got No Press). He hosted the long running Cobalt Café reading series in Canoga Park for almost twenty-one years, relaunched in 2020 as a virtual series, and has read his poetry all over the world.

Rick created *Poetry Super Highway*, an online resource and publication for poets (PoetrySuperHighway.com), *Haikuniverse*, a daily online small poem publication (Haikuniverse.com), and writes and occasionally draws the daily web comic *Cat and Banana* with Brendan Constantine. (facebook.com/catandbanana) He also writes the weekly Jewish poetry blog *From the Lupertverse* for JewishJournal.com

Rick works as a music teacher at synagogues in Southern California and as a graphic and web designer for anyone who would like to help pay his mortgage.

Rick's Other Books and Recordings

The Tokyo-Van Nuys Express
Ain't Got No Press ~ August, 2020

Hunka Hunka Howdee!
Ain't Got No Press ~ May, 2019

Beautiful Mistakes
Rothco Press ~ May, 2018

17 Holy Syllables
Ain't Got No Press ~ January, 2018

A Poet's Siddur: Friday Evening (edited by)
Ain't Got No Press ~ November, 2017

God Wrestler: A Poem for Every Torah Portion
Ain't Got No Press ~ August, 2017

Donut Famine
Rothco Press ~ December, 2016

Romancing the Blarney Stone
Rothco Press ~ December, 2016

Professor Clown on Parade
Rothco Press ~ December, 2016

Rick Lupert Live and Dead (Album)
Ain't Got No Press ~ March, 2016

Making Love to the 50 Ft. Woman
Rothco Press ~ May, 2015

The Gettysburg Undress
Rothco Press ~ May, 2014

Ekphrastia Gone Wild (edited by)
Ain't Got No Press ~ July, 2013

Nothing in New England is New
Ain't Got No Press ~ March, 2013

Death of a Mauve Bat
Ain't Got No Press ~ January, 2012

The Night Goes On All Night Noir Inspired Poetry
(edited by)
Ain't Got No Press ~ November, 2011

Sinzibuckwud!
Ain't Got No Press ~ January, 2011

We Put Things In Our Mouths
Ain't Got No Press ~ January, 2010

A Poet's Haggadah (edited by)
Ain't Got No Press ~ April, 2008

A Man With No Teeth Serves Us Breakfast
Ain't Got No Press ~ May, 2007

I'd Like to Bake Your Goods
Ain't Got No Press ~ January, 2006

Stolen Mummies
Ain't Got No Press ~ February, 2003

Brendan Constantine is My Kind of Town
Inevitable Press ~ September, 2001

Up Liberty's Skirt
Cassowary Press ~ March, 2001

Feeding Holy Cats
Cassowary Press ~ May, 2000

I'm a Jew, Are You?
Cassowary Press ~ May, 2000

Mowing Fargo
Sacred Beverage Press ~ December, 1998

Lizard King of the Laundromat
The Inevitable Press ~ February, 1998

I Am My Own Orange County
Ain't Got No Press ~ May, 1997

Paris: It's The Cheese
Ain't Got No Press ~ May, 1996

For more information:
www.PoetrySuperHighway.com